What Is the Coronavirus Disease COVID-19?

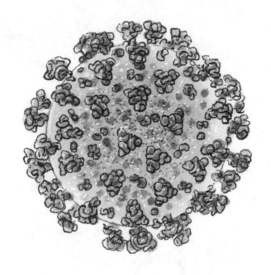

What Is
the Coronavirus
Disease COVID-19?

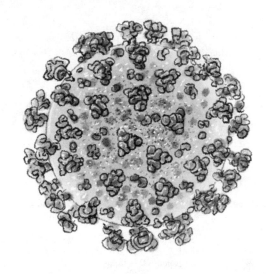

by Michael Burgan

illustrated by Manuel Gutierrez

Penguin Workshop

To the health-care professionals who have worked so
tirelessly to treat the victims of COVID-19—MB

PENGUIN WORKSHOP
An imprint of Penguin Random House LLC, New York

First published in the United States of America by Penguin Workshop, an imprint of
Penguin Random House LLC, New York, 2021

Visit us online at penguinrandomhouse.com.

Library of Congress Control Number: 2021011528

Printed in the United States of America

ISBN 9780593383612 (paperback)   10 9 8 7 6 5 4 3 2 1
ISBN 9780593383803 (library binding)   10 9 8 7 6 5 4 3 2 1

Contents

What Is the
Coronavirus Disease COVID-19?

In March 2020, people in New York City began to open their windows each evening at 7:00 p.m. Some stood on balconies and fire escapes. Then, they began to make a lot of noise. Some clanged on pots and pans. Others clapped their hands, sang, or played music.

All that noise had a purpose. New Yorkers, as well as people all over the United States and around the world, were in their homes, trying to stay safe. They wanted to show their support for essential workers and the doctors, nurses, and others who were working hard to fight a new virus that was spreading quickly. Health-care workers were treating the people who were very sick from the disease caused by the virus. At times, the doctors and nurses couldn't cure some of their patients. Hundreds of thousands died. What was this virus, and why was it such a threat to people in the United States and around the entire world?

CHAPTER 1
Viruses and Pandemics

Every day, we're surrounded by tiny particles that shape our lives. Some are living organisms called bacteria. Bacteria can be helpful—for example, ones in our stomach help digest our food. Other bacteria can cause disease. So can viruses, another kind of very tiny organism.

Unlike bacteria, viruses are not alive. But they do contain chemicals, like DNA, that help living things survive. Those chemicals are surrounded by a layer of protein. Although they aren't actually alive, viruses have a mission—to make copies of themselves. To do that, they need to invade the cells of an animal or a person.

Once inside the cells, a virus can damage or destroy them, which can in turn make a person sick. In the worst cases, the illnesses caused by the virus are deadly. The human body has a natural defense, called the immune system, that can attack invaders like bacteria and viruses. But when a new virus appears and infects people for the first time, their immune systems don't recognize the virus. They can't destroy the virus and stop it from spreading.

One common group of viruses is called coronaviruses. Under a microscope, they look like round balls covered with tiny spikes. Not all coronaviruses cause disease, but most people have felt the effects of some of them. Coronaviruses are the reason for the coughs, sniffles, and sneezes of the common cold.

Some harmful coronaviruses can spread quickly and infect many people in a particular region. This is called an epidemic. If the virus keeps spreading around the world, it creates what's called a pandemic. The virus that sickened so many in 2020 was a type of coronavirus. The disease it causes is called COVID-19. The coronavirus sparked one of the world's deadliest pandemics since the influenza outbreak of 1918.

When COVID-19 was first detected, scientists realized it was caused by a novel (which means "new") coronavirus—a virus that had never appeared in humans before. It's related to an earlier coronavirus that causes a disease called severe acute respiratory syndrome (SARS). Respiratory means it affects the lungs and other parts of the body that help people breathe. Because the coronavirus that appeared in 2019 was new, people's immune systems could not defend against it. That helped the virus spread quickly.

The Flu Pandemic of 1918

For centuries, a number of related viruses called influenza—flu for short—have sickened people around the world. These viruses lead to the disease we call "the flu." The flu and the health problems it can cause kill tens of thousands of people every year. Those numbers would be much higher, except people are able to get a flu vaccine to help prevent influenza. A vaccine is a treatment used to keep people from becoming sick.

But in 1918, there was no flu vaccine. When the influenza pandemic broke out, it lasted until 1919, and about five hundred million people were infected with the virus.

As many as fifty million people around the world died during the 1918 flu pandemic. Over time, the influenza virus slowly changed and

became less deadly. And people's immune systems began to work better against it. A vaccine wasn't developed until 1938. And it wasn't approved for the public until 1946.

CHAPTER 2
The Spread of COVID-19

The World Health Organization first announced that the world faced a threat from a new virus in January 2020. Reports from Wuhan, a city in China, described an outbreak of a sickness that had first appeared there in November 2019. Then, on January 11, Chinese officials said someone had died from the virus. By the end of the month, people in other countries were showing signs of the disease caused by the virus. The disease was named COVID-19, after 2019, the year it first appeared.

The Chinese government tried to stop the spread of COVID-19 by cutting off Wuhan from all outside contact. Trains and buses leaving the city were stopped and all flights grounded and airports closed. For the rest of the world, though, it was too late. People with COVID-19 had already traveled outside Wuhan, and the virus was spreading fast.

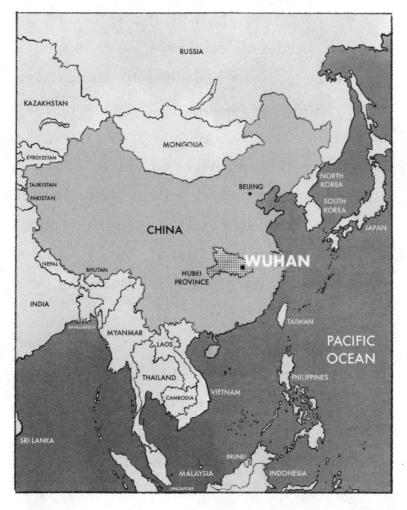

In February, the first COVID-19-related deaths outside China were recorded. Then the number of COVID-19 cases began to rise in several countries, especially in Italy and Iran. Governments tried to halt the spread of the disease by ordering lockdowns: Most businesses had to close, and people had to stay in their homes as much as possible. The lockdowns forced children to attend school online from home and adults to work remotely as well. But other people still had to report to work because their jobs were considered important. These "essential" workers included doctors and nurses, police officers, firefighters, delivery people, bus drivers, and workers in grocery stores.

By the end of February, about eighty thousand people around the world had been infected with the new coronavirus. In the middle of the month, US president Donald Trump said the spread of COVID-19 posed a serious threat to Americans' health and that the US government would give states $50 billion to fight the disease. Each state would create its own plan to handle the virus. They received advice from a government department called the Centers for Disease Control and Prevention (CDC).

Across the country, Americans began to fear for their health—and their jobs. The lockdowns forced many businesses to close. California became the first state to issue a lockdown, and other states quickly followed. The lockdowns were "stay-at-home" orders that forced people to stay where they were because of the risk.

The first steps to fight COVID-19 had little effect. By the end of March, the United States had more than eighty-three thousand COVID-19 cases—more than any other country. Many of the infected people lived in New York and New Jersey. Hospitals there began to fill with patients who were seriously ill from COVID-19.

Doctors and nurses began to run out of the masks and protective clothing they needed to shield themselves from the virus. By the end of

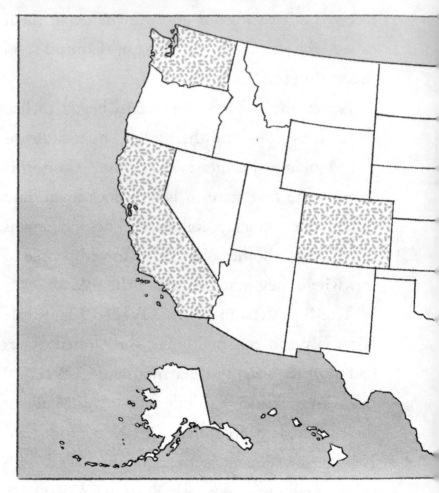

April, New York State was clearly the center of the pandemic in the United States, with more than eighteen thousand deaths.

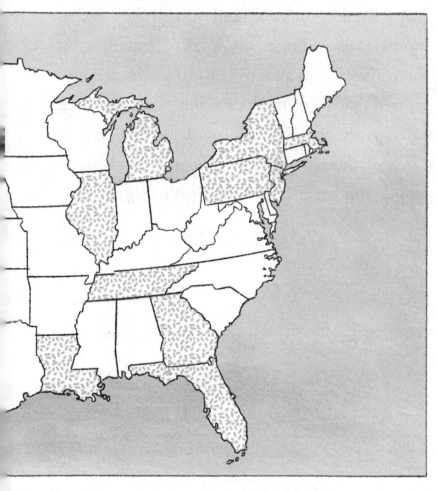

States with more than five hundred cases of COVID-19
as of March 12, 2020

Meanwhile, COVID-19 cases and deaths were rising in other states and around the world. The number of cases was high in many cities, where people lived, commuted, and worked close to one another. People hoped to protect themselves by buying face masks and using hand sanitizer. Some worried that stores might run out of supplies like toilet paper and food. They rushed to buy as much of these things as they could. And many people wondered: Could the virus be stopped?

CHAPTER 3
The Effects of COVID-19

Medical experts on infectious diseases and how they spread began studying COVID-19 soon after it was discovered. They tracked all the different symptoms, or signs, that the illness produced. Scientists also tried to find the best way to treat people who became sick with the disease.

At first, some doctors thought one way people could become infected was if they touched a surface that had the virus on it. The public was asked to wash their hands often and for at least twenty seconds. But by the middle of 2020, studies showed that most people didn't get sick by touching something that had the virus on it. The most common way to get COVID-19 was through the air.

When people breathe, speak, sing, or otherwise exhale air through their mouths and noses, they shoot out tiny bits of fluid called droplets. They come from the body's respiratory system. When people who have COVID-19 exhale, they can send out droplets carrying some of the virus. Any person near them is at risk of breathing in those droplets and getting sick.

Masks help reduce the spread of the virus

Some sick people have higher levels of the virus in their bodies and so can spread more of it through their droplets. The more time a healthy person spends close to a person who is sick, the higher their chances of getting sick, too. The risk goes up even more if people are close to one another indoors. In the spring of 2020, officials at the CDC began to suggest that people not gather in large groups, especially indoors or in buildings where there was not much fresh air. Scientists also said that people should try to stand at least six feet away from others. That "social distancing" would make it harder for the virus to spread. People were also encouraged to wear a mask that covered their mouth and nose when they were out in public and near other people.

By studying people who became sick from COVID-19, scientists learned that it can cause a long list of symptoms. Some are similar to the ones caused by influenza or the common cold: feeling tired and achy, having a cough or sore throat, or developing a fever. But as the pandemic spread, doctors saw more COVID-19 symptoms. The virus can cause headaches, stomach problems, and the loss of taste or smell. Some symptoms are signs that the illness is serious, such as having trouble breathing or pressure in the chest. Many COVID-19 patients who are admitted to hospitals develop even more severe health issues.

How sick someone gets from the coronavirus is based on several factors. It causes more serious illness in many elderly people and those with cancer, heart problems, and diabetes. Also at higher risk are pregnant women, smokers, and obese people. In general, men are more likely to die from serious cases of COVID-19 than women of the same age.

Research showed that people with COVID-19 have the greatest chance of infecting others starting two days before they first show symptoms. The odds of spreading the disease remain high for five days after the symptoms appear. During that period, it's especially important to keep infected people away from others. As COVID-19 spread, many countries enforced quarantines—fourteen-day isolation periods—for those who had the disease. That meant the sick person had to stay at home and avoid contact with anyone else. People who had been exposed to someone with the virus were told to isolate as well.

Trying to stop the spread of COVID-19 is challenging, since people carrying the virus can infect others before they have symptoms. Even worse, some infected people never show signs of the disease at all. They are called asymptomatic. About 30 percent of people who carry the virus are asymptomatic. As the pandemic spread, these people went to work or family gatherings not realizing they could spread the virus to others. Some large gatherings became known as "super-spreader" events—just one person sick with COVID-19 could infect many others in a short period. Those newly infected people would then leave the event and keep spreading the disease to others.

One curious thing the experts have noticed is that children are less likely to get severely sick from COVID-19. And the younger the children are, the more likely they are to have milder symptoms. Many children with COVID-19, though, are asymptomatic, and so can pass it on to others without realizing it.

CHAPTER 4
Finding and Treating the Sick

Scientists around the world took action. They developed tests for COVID-19 and began working on vaccines. The tests would show if someone was positive, meaning they had the virus and could spread it. The first tests were done in China in January 2020. As the virus spread around the world, the demand for tests increased. Some people had to wait in lines for several hours to get a test. But doctors agreed that doing even more testing was important to control the virus.

Health experts also stressed the need to learn who an infected person had been near while they were most likely to spread the virus. This is called contact tracing. The idea is to get these other people tested as soon as possible and to have them stay at home until they learn if they are positive for COVID-19. Contact tracing helps keep infected, and possibly infected, people away from others. Some countries had success with contact tracing, such as Germany and South Korea. Their efforts helped them contain the virus when the pandemic first began.

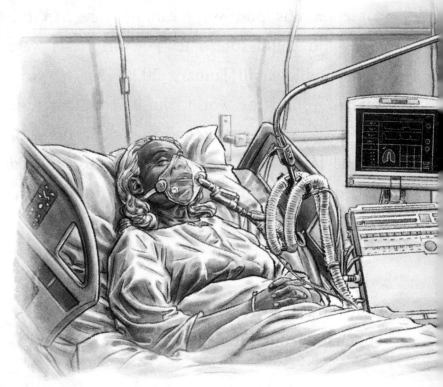

From the start of the pandemic, many of the sickest COVID-19 patients had serious trouble breathing. They were often hooked up to machines called ventilators. These machines helped them breathe. But even with the ventilators and care from specially trained nurses and doctors, many people died from COVID-19.

As the pandemic unfolded, doctors saw that certain people were affected by the virus more than others. In the United States and other countries, Black, indigenous, and people of color (BIPOC) were more likely to get COVID-19 and to die from it than white people. One CDC study found that Black and Hispanic children in the United States were five and eight times more likely to need hospital care than white children. Experts had several theories about why whites and people of color had different experiences with COVID-19. In the United States, people of color were less likely to have jobs that could be completed from home. They worked at businesses considered to be essential. That meant they had to be around many people during the day—and some of those people carried the virus.

BIPOC also often did not have access to proper medical care. The Navajo Nation in the

American Southwest was particularly hard hit by the virus. Many people there are so poor that they don't even have running water in their homes. The Navajo struggled to get medical care for sick people.

CHAPTER 5
The Cost of the Pandemic

As COVID-19 forced many countries and some US states to order lockdowns, the pandemic presented a new problem: The lockdowns were meant to keep people healthy, but they began to weaken the world's economy. The economy of a region is made up of all the goods and services people create and sell. In a healthy economy, most people can find work and afford to buy food, clothing, and housing. They might also have money to spend on entertainment or travel. For millions of people, all over the world, keeping their jobs and having enough money just to survive became difficult as the lockdowns began.

In the spring of 2020, the US government

acted quickly to try to boost the country's economy. A law passed near the end of March approved $2 trillion in aid. Some of the aid went directly to more than 150 million Americans, to spend any way they wanted. People who lost their jobs received $600 per week, along with money paid by each state. Businesses received money, too, and so did state and local governments. About $150 billion helped pay for medical equipment and hospital care across the country. Some people who rented their homes also received help. For four months, landlords could not force renters out of their homes if they couldn't pay their rent. Later, the CDC extended this protection for renters, and the government spent another $900 billion in COVID-19 aid.

Even with all that help, the US economy struggled. By May, about fourteen million people had lost their jobs, and the amount of goods and services produced fell sharply. Among the businesses that suffered most were restaurants, airlines, and hotels.

As the virus spread, some states began to require people to wear masks when they were in public spaces and could not stay at least six

feet away from others. The lockdowns, masks, and social distancing seemed to have some effect. By mid-May, the number of new positive cases of COVID-19 had fallen a bit from the peak numbers in April. Still, the virus had proven to be deadly. About one hundred thousand Americans had died since the first known case of COVID-19 in the country.

After the spring lockdowns, people wanted to live their lives as they had before the pandemic. State governors began to reopen some of the businesses they had closed earlier. Other states allowed large groups of people to gather again. Many people, some not wearing masks, spent time together over the Memorial Day weekend in late May, at parties, weddings, and other events.

The CDC and other medical experts, though, warned that the virus was still a threat. They said that the number of cases could increase again as more people spent time together without masks.

The experts were soon proven right. In July, the number of cases began to rise. The virus struck hard in states that had not had many cases in the spring. These included Texas, Florida, and Arizona. But governors there did not want to close stores or force people to wear masks. They feared the economies of their states would suffer if they implemented any of the suggested rules and restrictions.

States with the greatest number of COVID-19 cases, July 1, 2020

Starting in mid-September, the number of cases in the United States began to increase again. The virus was now hitting hard in rural states that had not seen many cases before, such as North Dakota. More governors began to require that people wear masks, and some began to put limits on businesses again. Those limits led to more job losses. By November, some twenty-six million people said they sometimes or often didn't have enough food to eat. Many waited in lines for hours to receive donations of food.

CHAPTER 6
The Politics of the Pandemic

From the start of the pandemic, US government leaders knew they faced a disease that could be deadly. But President Donald Trump and his advisers did not want to scare people about how serious COVID-19 was. At the same time, CDC officials wanted people to know the risks and take the proper steps to stop the spread of the virus. One of the top US health officials was Dr. Anthony Fauci. He and the president did not always agree on how the government should respond to the pandemic.

As the pandemic went on, Dr. Fauci and other health experts stressed the need for people to wear masks in public. President Trump, a

Dr. Anthony Fauci

Republican, refused to wear one in public until July. And he often didn't wear one when he was outside the White House after that. The president's supporters took this as a sign that they didn't need to wear masks, either. Some believed that being forced to wear a mask denied them their freedom. Some protested when their governors ordered them to wear masks or placed limits on which businesses could stay open.

Many Republican voters believed that the virus was not that dangerous. This was especially true in the states that hadn't seen many positive cases and deaths at the beginning of the pandemic. In the states that were impacted the most by early COVID-19 cases, the governors usually belonged to the other major US political party, the Democrats. In general, Democratic governors and city mayors acted quickly to order lockdowns and require that masks be worn in public.

They told residents that wearing a mask was a small price to pay to keep cities and states safe. Republican governors, however, were less likely to require masks. And when they did shut down some businesses, they moved quickly to end restrictions when the first wave of the pandemic seemed to ease.

The virus, though, did not recognize state borders. And governors and lawmakers from both major parties learned that the virus did not care about a person's politics. Leaders from both parties began to test positive for the virus. In October, the president and several members of his family tested positive for COVID-19.

The president was rushed to the hospital, where he received treatments that were still being tested and that were not available to most people. He recovered from the virus, but he seemed determined not to state publicly how serious a threat it was to the nation. And he was counting on future vaccines to help stop the spread of the virus.

On November 3, US voters elected Democrat Joe Biden to be their next president. He had a different view of the pandemic. Biden wore a mask every time he went out in public. He said that the government needed to listen to medical experts like Dr. Fauci. And he wanted to give more money to the states to fight the pandemic. Biden also knew that as president, he would have limited powers to require everyone to wear a mask. But he supported the governors who did, and who were ready to shut down some businesses to control the pandemic.

By December 2020, many countries saw a huge second wave of the virus. In the United States, the number of cases per day broke records. Some days, more than two hundred thousand people tested positive. The number of deaths began to go up again, too—sometimes more than three thousand each day. Political leaders around the world still had to deal with the health dangers and economic problems caused by COVID-19.

CHAPTER 7
The Future with COVID-19

By the end of 2020, the United States led the world in the number of positive cases of COVID-19 and deaths caused by the virus. Almost twenty million Americans had tested positive, out of a total of more than eighty million worldwide. About 350,000 Americans had already died, out of a worldwide total of more than 1.5 million deaths. By the time President Joe Biden took office in January 2021, more Americans had died of COVID-19 than in World Wars I and II, the Vietnam War, and the September 11 attacks combined. Some US states, such as New York, Texas, and California, had more than twenty-five thousand deaths each—higher totals than in dozens of individual countries.

Throughout the pandemic, some nations had been able to slow the spread by taking strong measures early on. New Zealand, for example, ordered a strict lockdown in March that closed most businesses and shut down or limited transportation for almost two months. People just stayed home. The country also made foreign visitors stay in special hotels for two weeks to be certain they were healthy. With these steps, New Zealand had fewer than twenty-five deaths by the end of 2020, out of a population of about five million people.

China, where the pandemic began, also put in place strict lockdown orders, and most citizens wore masks in public. A country of more than 1.4 billion people, China had fewer than five thousand COVID-19 deaths by the end of 2020. With its strong effort to contain the virus, China was one of the few countries in the world that saw their economies grow in 2020.

Finland and Norway had similar success in containing the virus, due to strict quarantines and contact tracing.

With the new year of 2021, people around the world hoped they had finally slowed the spread of the virus. Health-care workers and the elderly were among the first groups to receive the new vaccines that had been approved by the

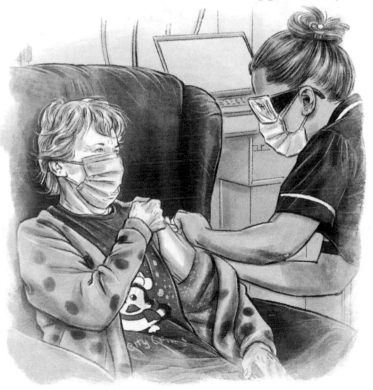

end of 2020. And by the middle of the year, hundreds of millions of doses of the vaccines were ready for use and being distributed worldwide.

But even as vaccines are distributed, the virus is having a lasting effect on how people live and work. More businesses have given workers the option to work from home. Millions of people began to buy groceries and the things they needed

online, rather than in stores. Many will keep shopping that way after the pandemic. Doctors began seeing many patients online during the pandemic, and many continued to even when COVID-19 was no longer a threat.

And what about schools? In general, students in grades kindergarten through twelve who began to learn online returned to their classrooms.

Studies showed that many students spent less time on schoolwork when learning remotely. Online learning also made many students feel lonely, easily distracted, and unhappy. Going forward, local leaders will have to act quickly if a new coronavirus outbreak happens, putting protective measures in place and requiring students and teachers to wear masks as well as practice social distancing.

Before 2020, many medical experts warned that a pandemic caused by a novel coronavirus could seriously affect both people's health and the world's economy. COVID-19 proved them right. Scientists don't know for sure how long the coronavirus will affect the global population. But vaccines and stronger steps at prevention have helped to slow the pandemic that struck the world in 2020.

Timeline of the Coronavirus Disease COVID-19

1918–1919	A flu pandemic kills about fifty million people worldwide
1946	The first flu vaccine is distributed to the public
2019	The first cases of COVID-19 are documented in Wuhan, China
Jan. 2020	The first known death from the virus is reported in China
	The first tests to detect the disease are produced
Feb. 2020	The first deaths attributed to COVID-19 occur outside China
Mar. 2020	Lockdowns begin in the US, as the government spends $2 trillion in aid
Apr. 2020	New York is the center of the pandemic in the United States, as more than eighteen thousand people have already died across the state
Jul. 2020	After most lockdowns had ended, COVID-19 cases slowly begin to rise again
Oct. 2020	The US government approves a medicine to treat patients with COVID-19
Dec. 2020	US deaths from COVID-19 surpass the high numbers reported in the spring, with more than three thousand deaths reported on some days
	Vaccines for COVID-19 are approved
Jan. 2021	Joe Biden becomes the forty-sixth US president and calls for tough measures to fight the coronavirus

Timeline of the World

1918 — World War I ends in Europe

1929 — The world's economy starts to weaken badly as the Great Depression begins

1939 — World War II starts in Europe

1964 — Ford shows off a new car, the Mustang, at the World's Fair in New York City

1976 — Apple begins selling its first computer

1981 — A virus called HIV begins to spread in the United States, and diseases it causes eventually kill millions of people around the world before scientists develop treatments for it

1994 — Thanks to a vaccine, polio, an infectious disease that sometimes causes paralysis, is eliminated from North and South America

2001 — Terrorists launch several attacks in the United States, killing almost three thousand people

2008 — Barack Obama is elected the first Black president of the United States

2019 — *Avengers: Endgame* makes more money around the world than any other movie in history

2021 — Kamala Harris becomes the first Black, South Asian American, and female vice president of the United States

Bibliography

*Books for young readers

"A Timeline of COVID-19 Developments in 2020." *The American Journal of Managed Care*. Last modified January 1, 2021. https://www.ajmc.com/view/a-timeline-of-covid19-developments-in-2020.

Barry, John M. *The Great Influenza: The Story of the Deadliest Pandemic in History*. New York: Penguin, 2005.

*Brown, Don. *Fever Year: The Killer Flu of 1918*. Boston: Houghton Mifflin Harcourt Books for Young Readers, 2019.

*Burgan, Michael. *Developing Flu Vaccines*. Chicago: Raintree, 2011.

"Coronavirus Coverage." *National Geographic*. https://www.nationalgeographic.com/science/coronavirus-coverage/.

"Coronavirus Disease (COVID-19) Pandemic." *World Health Organization*. https://www.who.int/emergencies/diseases/novel-coronavirus-2019.

"COVID-19." *Centers for Disease Control and Prevention*. https://www.cdc.gov/coronavirus/2019-nCoV/index.html.

*Hodgkins, Fran. *Finding a Covid-19 Vaccine*. San Diego: BrightPoint Press, 2021.

"Influenza (Flu)." *Centers for Disease Control and Prevention*. https://www.cdc.gov/flu/index.htm.

"Novel Pandemics." *Ready.gov*. Last modified November 12, 2020. https://www.ready.gov/pandemic.

Shah, Sonia. *Pandemic: Tracking Contagions, from Cholera to Ebola and Beyond*. New York: Picador, 2017.

"The Coronavirus Outbreak." *New York Times*. https://www.nytimes.com/news-event/coronavirus?name=styln-coronavirus&region=TOP_BANNER&block=storyline_menu_re circ&action=click&pgtype=LegacyCollection&impression_id=7bfe5970-6032-11eb-a4fa-255a772ef6ao&variant=1_Show.

Zakaria, Fareed. *Ten Lessons for a Post-Pandemic World*. New York: W. W. Norton, 2020.

YOUR HEADQUARTERS FOR HISTORY

Activities, Mad Libs, and sidesplitting jokes!
Discover the Who HQ books beyond the biographies

Based on the New York Times Best-Selling Series

Knock! Knock! Who Was There?

OVER 300 sidesplitting jokes

by Brian Elling

Based on the New York Times Best-Selling Series

Knock! Knock! Where Is There?

OVER 300 sidesplitting jokes

by Brian Elling

The Who Was? Activity Book

Puzzles, Mazes, & Tons of Fun

Based on the New York Times Best-Selling Series

From The New York Times best-selling Who Was? Series

Who Is _____? The Story of My Life

A Journal for You, by You!

by Paula K. Manzanero

Who Was? MAD LIBS

World's Greatest Word Game

Who? What? Where?

Learn more at whohq.com!